KIRKBY O.

A LINCOLNSHI

—— 1900-2000 ——

by Molly Burkett
and the children of Kirkby on Bain School

Words © Molly Burkett

ISBN N° 1 903172 06 3

Published by Barny Books
Hough on the Hill, Grantham, Lincolnshire

Produced by: **TUCANN***design&print*, 19 High Street, Heighington, Lincoln LN4 1RG
Telephone and Fax: 01522 790009

This book is dedicated to the memory of
Oliver Lacey
1990-1999
"He would have enjoyed contributing to this book"

KIRKBY ON BAIN – 1900

My cousin came to visit and she said that she'd walked right through the village and she hadn't seen a soul. That tells you how much life in Kirkby on Bain has changed. There were always people about, people in the village and people working in the fields. They didn't have the machines that they have today. Everything had to be done by hand. Farms were different too. They were smaller, mostly family run and they didn't specialise. They did a bit of everything, grew a few crops and vegetables, kept a few cows, pigs and hens and a couple of heavy horses. Life seemed slower. People had time to stop and talk. My mother said it used to take her an hour to go and fetch a loaf of bread by the time she had passed the time of day with the baker and stopped to talk to the people she met along the way.

Farming was labour intensive. Men and horses did the many jobs on the land that machines do today. You could pick up casual work on the farm. I earned my first money picking up stones and putting them in a basket at the end of the row. Itinerant workers came through looking for work. The Irish came over when it was time to pull the beet, and stayed for the potato harvest. It was all done by hand. They were real hard workers but they were rough and they could swear. Mother used to shut the windows when she heard them out in the lane but we heard everything they said even if we did pretend to be asleep.

After the First World War, it was old soldiers that came through looking for work. They had come back from fighting and found there were no jobs for them. Some of then had been wounded and didn't have a day's work in them. We thought about our own lads that hadn't come home. We tried to make sure we had something to give them even if there wasn't any work.

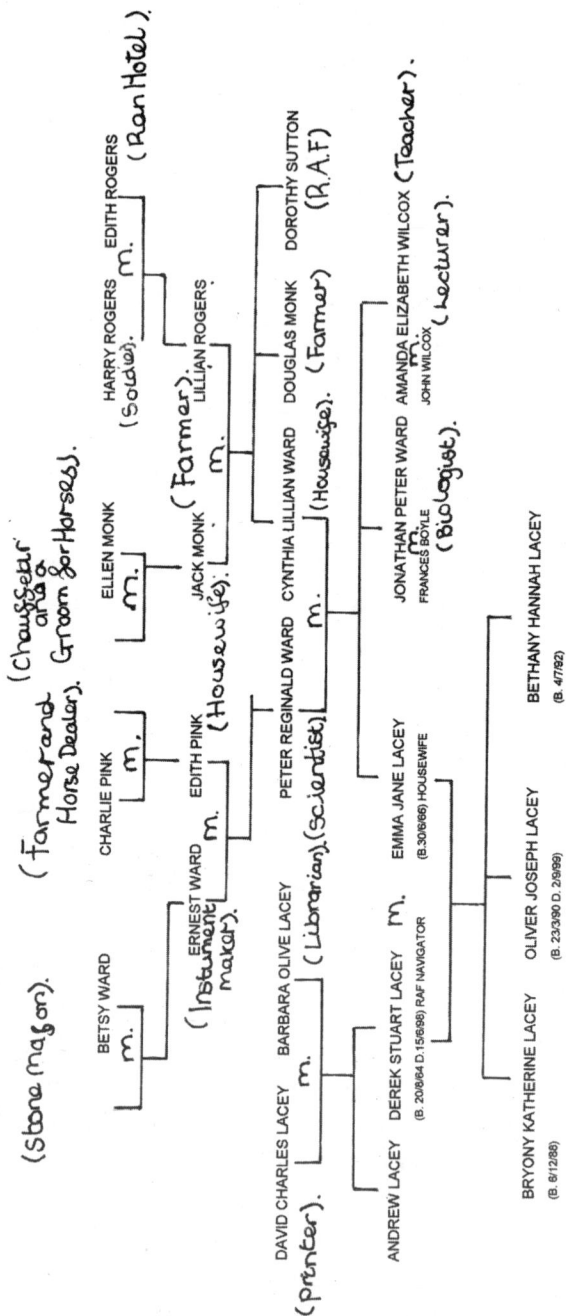

BETSY WARD
m.
(Stone mason).

CHARLIE PINK
m.
(Farmer and Horse Dealer).

ELLEN MONK
m.
(Chauffeur and a Groom for Horses).

HARRY ROGERS
(Soldier).
m.
EDITH ROGERS
(Ran Hotel).

ERNEST WARD
(Instrument maker).
m.
EDITH PINK
(Housewife).

JACK MONK (Farmer).
m.
LILLIAN ROGERS

DOUGLAS MONK
(Farmer)
m.
DOROTHY SUTTON
(R.A.F)

PETER REGINALD WARD
(Scientist)
m.
CYNTHIA LILLIAN WARD
(Housewife).

JONATHAN PETER WARD
(Biologist).
m.
FRANCES BOYLE

AMANDA ELIZABETH WILCOX (Teacher).
m.
JOHN WILCOX
(Lecturer).

DAVID CHARLES LACEY
(printer).
m.
BARBARA OLIVE LACEY
(Librarian).

EMMA JANE LACEY
(B.30/6/66) HOUSEWIFE

ANDREW LACEY

DEREK STUART LACEY
(B. 20/8/64 D.15/6/98) RAF NAVIGATOR
m.

BRYONY KATHERINE LACEY
(B. 8/12/88)

OLIVER JOSEPH LACEY
(B. 23/3/90 D. 2/9/99)

BETHANY HANNAH LACEY
(B. 4/7/92)

Horse drawn cart

Horse drawn plough

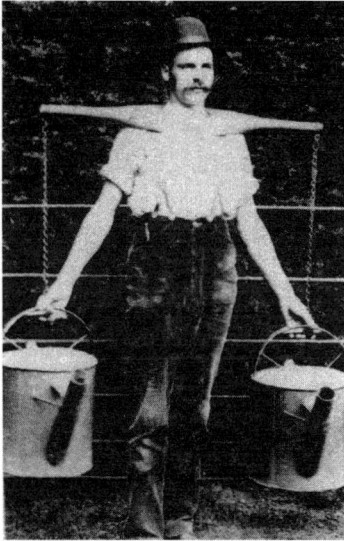

Water Carrier

Tramps came through the village and they were hungry. They were hungry times. The Romanies visited Kirby at the same time every year and stayed awhile with their horse drawn caravans and what seemed like crowds of children and horses. I was a bit frightened of them. The men would do some work at the farms and the women made clothes pegs and made ointments from the wild plants. When I had earache, mother fetched some ointment from the gypsy. I don't know what was in it but it cured my earache.

It was the depression then. That was a bad time for everyone, no work and no money for a lot of people. We weren't too badly off in Kirkby. We could live off the land to a certain extent. There were rabbits and pigeons for the pot. Most of us grew our own vegetables and had a few hens.

We had our own farm and we were self reliant with milk and butter as well. In a small community like Kirkby, we would look after our own needy. I can't remember any of the old folk who couldn't work any longer having to go into the workhouse at Horncastle but I know that there were plenty who did.

The farmers were hit as badly as the men who worked for them. I can remember seeing men sitting on the verge waiting for the farmer to come back from market, hoping that he would have made enough money to be able to pay them their wages.

Ted Brader was the blacksmith. He lived in Lilac Cottage next to the chapel. He'd taken over from John Watson when he got too old to carry on. We used to stop and watch him on the way home from school. He always had time to talk. Jackie Sharp was the joiner and wheelwright and it was fascinating to see him work, making the big wheels for the farm carts. He lived with his sister. He never married. Cliff Scarborough was the cobbler. He was always busy. People looked after their shoes and boots. Most of us only had the one pair. There wasn't the money to buy anything that we could do without. If you could afford it, Cliff could make you a pair of shoes or boots but there weren't many

The Village Shop

that could afford that luxury. Mrs. Pinning ran the grocery shop, then Mr. and Mrs. Prime ran it. Later Mr. Milne took it over and his daughter ran it when her father died. She had to close it in 1992 and look for other employment because she was no longer able to make a living from it. Villagers preferred to shop at supermarkets. There had been a shop on that site for 150 years.

Miss Milne still lives in the house and Phyllis Underwood still lives at the old post office which she ran for fifty-six years. When she retired in 1996, nobody would take it over. We have to go into Haltham now. There's a post office

Mud and Stud Cottage

that's open two mornings a week or we have to wait until we go into town.

The coal merchant was in the mill yard alongside the bakers. I worked at the bakers when I left school. The grindstones were still in place when I started but they were taken out in 1940. The mill had been in use until 1930's. Arthur Wells was the baker when I started but he was drowned in the mill pool in 1940. He'd been crossing the bridge and had kicked out at a rat, lost his balance and fell into the river. Mr. Chester took over then.

Mr. Roberts would light the coke fire on the Sunday evening to get the oven

The Watermill

warm. I would be out of the house by five o'clock and along to the bakehouse for an early start. Flour, salt, yeast and hot water was measured out and mixed for half an hour to make the dough. Then we put the dough in a trough in front of the oven to rise and I went home for my breakfast. When I got back, the dough was put on a bench and cut and weighed into two pound loaves. These were kneaded and folded into the tins. Some of the tins had lids on them for the steam loaves. Then they were put in the oven and baked for an hour. The smell of the baking bread was wonderful. It used to make me feel hungry even though I'd only just had my breakfast. It's one of the smells I remember of my childhood, the smell of the baking bread. Then we would load the bread and deliver it. We delivered three times a week in the village and twice a week round the local areas. We had a van. A loaf of bread was fourpence, buns and jam tarts were a penny each, and sponges were one shilling and sixpence. We used milk powder for the milk bread and egg powder for the cakes. We made Christmas cakes on the Sunday before Christmas when the ovens were out. Some housewives who had made their own cakes would often bring them to the baker to cook in his oven.

There were plenty of tradesmen that came round. The coalman delivered and so did the milkman. He started delivering milk to the village when milk was rationed in the war. Until then farmers supplied the milk in Kirkby. Before the Second World War Mrs. Spikins and Mrs. Underwood delivered the milk on their bikes, balancing the churns on their handlebars. They had pint measures with long metal handles which they would dip into the milk and pour the required measure into the housewives' jugs. They fetched the milk from Lockwood's farm and charged twopence a pint. In Thimbleby people used to take their

The Milkman

jugs and go up to the farm and collect their own milk. It was still warm when they took it home.

I had to get up early and deliver the milk before I went to school. Sometimes I had to take the cows back to the field before I started on my round. One day Miss. Brader came out with a colander and expected me to put the milk in that.

Now our milk is delivered by a battery driven milk float. It doesn't come every day because not everyone in the village buys their milk from the milkman. They prefer to buy it at the supermarket. They say it's cheaper.

Mr. Shin used to come round with the dray bringing groceries and Lukes the butchers from Coningsby used to come round with the van. We didn't have a butcher in the village then because country people didn't eat that much shop meat. We would have a joint on Sunday but we'd get by with fat bacon in the week and rabbits of course. Rabbits were there for the taking. Rabbit meat was a staple diet.

Mr. Archer came round with his dray every Tuesday selling brushes and crockery and Joe Callingham used to come on his bike every Friday afternoon. He would sell brushes and dusters, which he had tied to his crossbar, but he would buy rabbit skins, twopence a time. Charlie Betts reckoned he furnished his house when he got married from the money he made from selling rabbit skins.

In the 1940's, there was a War Agricultural policy to control the rats. Rats were a real problem. I only saw a rat migration once. I heard them first, rustling through the undergrowth, squeaking, squealing. They swarmed over everything that got in their way. Nothing would stop them. It was like an avalanche of rats. We collected the rats' tails when we killed them and took them to Kemps up North Street in Horncastle and got 2d. each for them.

The Second World War changed so many things. It was difficult to import food and we had to produce our own. Farming was essential and farmworkers were not allowed to join up. They were too valuable working on the land. The Ministry of Agriculture saw that every effort was made to produce food. If a farmer was not doing well he was likely to be turned out and a more

Grinter was a German Prisoner of War who worked on Spikings Farm

efficient farmer put in his place. We were encouraged to grow more crops and use more land. Land that we would not have ploughed was ploughed then for the war effort. Land girls were billeted in the village at Top Park Farm. They livened things up. We had POWs (Prisoners of War) working on the land. They were brought down by bus each day from their camp but we needed help over the weekend so we had one stopping on the farm. He lived in the shed but he ate with the family. We were much of an age and we got on real well. He was called Grinter and I often wonder what happened to him. We kept in touch for a long time but then his letters stopped coming.

Off duty airmen and soldiers used to come and give a hand. They were always ready to earn a bit extra. There were several airfields round here. Coningsby and Tattershall Thorpe were the nearest. It's difficult to explain what it was like in the war years but there always seemed to be aeroplanes in the air and they weren't always ours. Kirkby was bombed one night. There were seven bombs landed on the village but no-one was badly hurt. Mrs. Leech at the post office had her arm broken and a horse in Mr. Atkin's field has some shrapnel in its thigh but the chapel had a direct hit and was demolished and so was the cottage at the end of Wharf Lane. The young couple had been in bed when the bombs dropped and they were rolled right out of bed and finished up on the riverbank, but they weren't hurt. George Thornley had this M.G. car and it was the pride of his life. He couldn't drive it in the war because he didn't have the petrol coupons but he got it out and went for help. He'd only gone half a mile when he realised all his tyres were flat but he still went and fetched help.

One Sunday morning, there was a plane came down in the field beyond the park, a Hampden. We went running when we heard the crash but there was nothing we could do. It had burst into flames. It was a fireball. The crew was burned to death. A Lancaster returning from a raid in Germany, landed in a field at Roughton. My father always reckoned the pilot mistook the river for the runway and tried to land on it. The whole crew was killed.

We were pretty self reliant in the village. We didn't need to go into Horncastle that often although my parents went in in the 1920's to get their shopping each week. They used to push me in my pram eight miles each way and think nothing of it. We didn't get a bus service in the village until 1953 and that was only on Saturdays. We could catch it to get in for the first showing at the pictures, have a fish and chip tea and catch the bus home. We had plenty of fun in the village. We were a community then. Church was part of our week each Sunday and we

A Lincolnshire Village

Jim and Dorothy Wright's 21st birthday party gathering in the Church Hall in 1956.

Dorothy died recently in 1999 and Jim still lives in Kirkby on Bain.

Kirkby School pupils at a confirmation service. Lawrence Major on the right was the son of Ethel Major who murdered her husband and was hung at Hull in 1934

Pupils at Kirkby on Bain School in the playground about 1970.

Lady on the right is headmistress Miss Matt. Mrs Dixon (dark haired lady in centre) was the school caretaker and still is today.

St Mary's Church

Church Garden Party

went to Sunday school, then we could go on the Sunday School outing to Skegness. That was the only time we saw the sea. We didn't have holidays. When we went on the bus to Skeggy, we always had salmon sandwiches. That was a real treat. We never had tinned food except as a special treat. I went to the Methodist Chapel and we had our outing to Skegness but we also went to Woodhall Spa by horse and cart and we would sing and collect at the big houses and when we got back we always had plum cake, seed cake, bread and butter tea. My Dad was cross when he found out that my brother used to go to both Sunday Schools, turn and turn about so that he could have two Sunday School outings.

A lot of men working on the farms were casual workers. When they didn't work or when there was no work for them to do, they didn't get paid. We were fortunate. My father was in regular employment. He was a foreman on a farm at Roughton. I went to school there. You stayed at the primary school until you were 14. The school's closed now and the children from the village come to

Potato Pickers

Kirkby School. We were expected to help when we got home from school and during the war we had brown cards and could take time off school if we were needed to help on the farm. There were any number of jobs we were expected to do, picking potatoes and pulling carrots or peas. We got three shillings a bag for peas. There was stone picking to do and singling the beet and there was always weeding. You didn't have weedkillers like they do today.

Everyone helped with the harvest and with the potato lifting. We had an extra holiday from school at the end of September to help with that.

We grew our own vegetables and we kept our own hens for eggs. We had our own cow for milk and we always had a pig in the sty. During the war we were allowed to have two pigs, one of which we kept for ourselves and the other was taken by the Ministry of Agriculture. It was always an occasion when it was time to kill the pig. The lady next door would go and stay at her sister's when they killed their pig. She always grew fond of it.

My father always killed his own pig but most of the neighbours would get the butcher from Coningsby to come and kill theirs. Father had a sharp knife tied firmly on the end of a stick and he would cut the pig's throat. He did it so quickly you hardly noticed it. No, I don't think it was cruel. It never worried me. It was the way of life. The pig was bled to make the meat sweet. Then the carcass was put in a copper of boiling water and the bristles were scraped off with sharp knives. Then it was opened up and the innards removed. The intestines were thoroughly washed and later used for sausage skins. The apron was used for the haslet. The carcass was then hung on a tripod to set (cool). The next day it was jointed, 2 hams, 2 shoulders, 2 flicks, chines and spare ribs. The big chine was saved and stuffed with parsley to eat at Mayday or a family christening.

14

Pea pullers at Roughton with Mr Tomlinson, haulage owner, in the centre.
On this photo is Betty Dixon and her father. Each worker received 3 shillings a 4 stone bag as shown.

Potato pickers at Roughton 1949-52.
Left to right: Mr Fawcett, Mrs Podham, ?, Mrs Allan, Betty Dixon, Joan Southwell, ?, Mrs Hawkins

Old farm machinery and traction engines

Pigs

Bernard Roberts with one of Mr Underwood's prize pigs. Bernard worked for Mr Underwood

Then the meat was salted, one ounce of saltpeter to four pounds of salt, to preserve it. There weren't refrigerators or deep freezers then. The salt came in blocks and we had to cut it down. That could make you hands sore especially if you had a cut on them. We made sausages and pork pies and used the red meat for haslets. The fry meat (liver and kidneys) was put through the sausage machine. The white kells (fat) was rendered down for lard. The feet, ears, bones and tail were boiled down for brawn. There wasn't a thing left of the pig except for the squeal.

My Grandad used to keep pigs at the bottom of his garden when he was a little boy. He'd had one that he used to let out of the sty and it would follow him round like a dog. He cried when the butcher came to kill it.

• • • • • •

Spoken by Rev. Cecil Surtees about John Sharpe who died in 1952 :
A few days ago I tolled the Church bell eighty five times. The ancient Parish Clerk, Sexton, Sideman, and Martha-of-all-work was no more. While I tolled the bell I tried to imagine the changes that had come over the small village in which he had spent a lifetime. In 1802 the first vessels were launched on the newly canalised River Bain, the Horncastle Navigation. Sometime about 1890 the last barge stuck in the village, unable to move for lack of water. The canal had been ruined by the competition of the Horncastle to Kirkstead Railway; opened in 1855.

The old man had grown up in those years when the population of the village had been doubled by boatwrights, rope makers and navvies. He remembered the barges slowly sailing through the village carrying coal or grain between the ancient port of Boston and the coalfields of the North and Midlands.

It was an era in which horses and carriages stood in the Rectory stables and such people as grooms and butlers are mentioned in the Church registers. The servants and the village children sat in a gallery in the Church.

During succeeding years one thinks of the gradual cutting of the domestic staff. The war passed. The servant's wing of the rectory was let off as a separate house.

Jet planes shriek over the quiet pastures now. We buried the old man yesterday;

he would have laughed could he have heard the disgruntled immigrants grumbling, "Nothing ever happens here."

• • • • • •

My Grandad is a pig farmer. He keeps Landrace pigs crossed with large whites. A female pig starts breeding at eight months when it is known as a gilt. When she has reared her first litter, she is called a sow. The piglets are taken away from their mother at 40 days and weaned. A good sow should rear twenty-five piglets a year.

• • • • • •

My father is a pig farmer but he's thinking of giving up and finding another job. The problem is that the bottom has fallen out of the market. He has to pay out more for their food than he can get for the pigs when he sells them at market. People still eat pork and bacon but the supermarkets prefer to buy a lot of their meat from abroad because they say it is cheaper. It may not be the same quality but they can produce it more cheaply in other countries because their farmers do not have the same restrictions that ours do. British farmers are not allowed to feed bone meal which comes from ground up carcasses. They have to use replacement concentrates instead and they are expensive. Pig farmers in Britain have to meet lots of regulations set by the Government and organisations like the Farm Assured British Pigs and the Molten Code. A lot of these are to do with animal welfare, for example there has to be one drinker for every ten animals and there must be no sharp edges in their sheds. Pigs reared abroad do not have these restrictions. Their pigs can be fed on feed which is not acceptable in Britain. They do not have to meet such stringent welfare standards so they can produce cheaper pork. The British farmer can produce quality food and safe pork but then cannot compete in price. The imported meat is unfair competition. We've never objected to imports but we want the quality of imported food to be of the same standard as we produce in our own country.

I am Emma Garner. My father is a farmer. We have 60 cows producing 50 calves a year for beef. We grow 600 acres of cereal and we have 200 ewes.

We put the rams to the ewes in August. The ewes have a 5 month pregnancy when they have a 16% protein, cereal based diet. They are brought inside into the lambing sheds at Christmas. Their feed has been gradually increased to 1 kilogram daily. They are also fed hay and fodder beet.

The lambs are given a cereal feed at 3 weeks. They are taken out of the sheds into pens in March where they feed apart from their mothers.

By Easter some lambs are large enough to be slaughtered. The better ones are kept for flock replacement or sold to other farmers.

• • • • • •

My grandfather was a sheep farmer. He used to buy a flock of sheep in the market, shear them, sell the wool and take them back to market the next week and sell them at the price he had paid for them. He made a good profit from the wool. You got a decent price for wool fifty years ago but there isn't any money in it now. People do not wear woollen clothes. They prefer man-made fibres. They're easier to launder and cheaper to manufacture. A fleece is worth 60 pence today. It doesn't cover the cost of shearing them but you have to do it for the animals' well-being.

I gave up keeping sheep twelve years ago. There's a lot of work in sheep and not enough profit in them. People think they only eat grass but they need supplements to their diet and they are expensive. My grandfather used to treat the animals himself but we always called in the vet and his charges and the medication all add to the cost.

• • • • • •

I left school when I was fourteen and went into service at Woodhall Spa. I looked after the children mainly. I cycled there and back each day and I had a half-day off each weekend. I soon gave that up. I found those that were working on the land were being paid more than I was so I went back to working on the farm.

We were expected to follow the same trade as our parents. There wasn't the education or opportunities that children have today. When I married I gave up work. Married women didn't work. They were too busy keeping house for their husbands. Working on the land was labour intensive so was managing a home. Washing seemed to take all week. Bob would get the copper going on a Monday morning to heat the water for the wash before he went off to work. We didn't have any hot water in the cottage. We didn't have any water. I used to fetch all that was needed from the pump and when that ran dry as it often did in a dry summer, I would fetch water from the well at the farm. We didn't get main water in until 1952. Then we only had a cold water pipe outside and it froze up as soon as the weather turned cold. We had the tap brought indoors and we had the old privy taken out and a proper toilet with a chain put in its place. We were one of the first to have a toilet put in. It was still outside mind you. People used to call on us and ask if they could use it. It was a treat to pull the chain and have everything washed away. Until then, Mike had had to go moonlighting on a Friday night, emptying the contents of the bucket in a hole he had ready down the garden. It helped the marrows grow. That was what he reckoned. Even when we had water indoors, it was only cold water, so I still had to heat the copper for the washing and use the dolly tub and the blue to make the whites white and the washboard to get the collars clean and the big old mangle to press out the moisture. I used to starch Mike's shirts and he used to moan if I made them too stiff. Then we used those old flat irons on the clothes. We heated them up on the fire but you had to be careful. The handle could be as hot as the

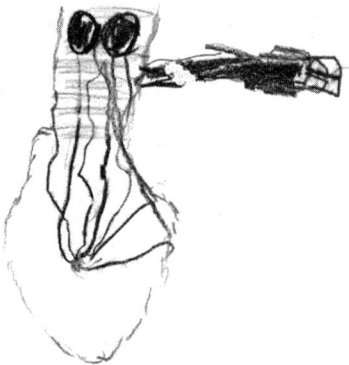

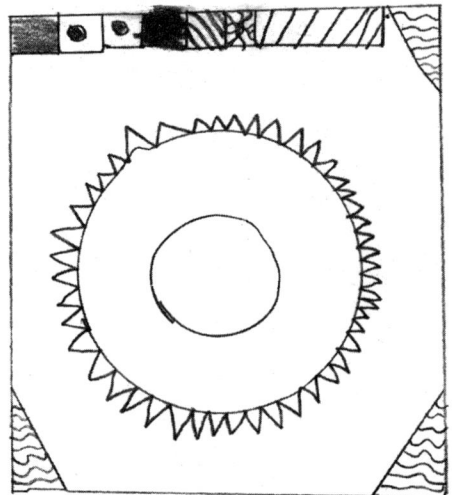

Electric lamp and Washing Machine

part that did the work. If it was damp weather, we had problems airing the clothes. I had an airer that I could pull up to the ceiling and I aired my clothes on that. I'd never heard of washing machines. We had electricity in in 1953 but we only used it for lighting at first. It was 1974 before I had a washing machine, one of those twin tubs.

You have no idea the difference that electricity made. It made the days longer for a start. We had used candles and pressure lamps for lighting. There were mantles on the lamps and they became brittle so if you didn't light them carefully, you could break the mantle. We used Tilley lamps in the yard. They hissed when they were alight. They were very bright but they didn't light up a very big area. During the war, my father bought a generator from the dispersal yard at Woodhall Spa.

My parents had a farm in Southwell, near Nottingham. They had a tenancy on the land and there was no security for tenants in those days, so they looked around for something they could buy and that was how we came down to this part of Lincolnshire. Moving was a problem. My father sold a lot of the stock and bought fresh nearer our new farm. The problem of that was that the cows arrived at the farm before we did but our new neighbour milked them for us and kept the milk in way of payment. We had to get a permit to move the stock. The cattle went by cattle truck and the rest by rail. Well, the trucks turned up early and they made such a noise that they sent the horses into a panic. They almost kicked the stable to pieces. My dad said we couldn't leave them like that so the two of us went down to deal with them. We put halters on them and calmed them down, then we lead them to the station. Dad and I went down with the lorry to settle the animals and when our neighbours realised we were camping out in an empty house, they insisted we stayed with them. My mother came down on the Friday with the furniture and we moved into the house. It took us a while to settle and find our way around. Everyone was friendly and helpful and we soon began to feel that we'd never lived anywhere else.

We didn't sell milk to the public but the men working on the farm were allowed to take two pints of milk home a day. We used to see our neighbour's herdsman cycling to the farm, morning and evening with his milk can on his handlebars. The milk cans held two pints and the farmer was always complaining that he was taking twice as much milk as he was entitled to. All the time we were there, this argument went on between the two of them and I don't think it was ever resolved.

My job when I came home from school was to pump the water up into the tank above the cowshed. The cows had special bowls called Fordham tongue operated drinking bowls. They had a lever which, when the cows pushed them with their tongues, would allow the water to flow down from the tank so that they could drink. It was a boring job, pumping up the water and seemed to go on for ever. I would do fifty pumps with one arm, then fifty with the other and so on. I'd long left school by the time they brought water into the village in the 1950s and we had a tap in the yard – no more carrying water for the animals – bliss!

We had Jersey cows at first and they gave really rich milk. The cream would come half way down the bottle. We'd never heard of low fat milk in those days and I don't think any of the farming folk would have drunk it if they had. Then in 1950 my father changed to Ayrshires. They're big strong animals with big horns. I took some cattle cake in to the shed and one of the cows turned and her horn caught me on the head above the eye and it swelled up like a balloon. I went to the doctor's and he gave me a tetanus injection. Tetanus was a worry in this part of the country, still is but you're injected against it now. The very next day, one of the cows horned the animal in front of it and cut it badly. She wasn't being vicious, they had got too close to each other. That was it. My father had the vet up the next day and had them all dehorned. Now the calves are dehorned with dehorning fluid when they are young.

The advantages of having Ayrshires was that A.I. (Artificial Insemination) had come in. We simply had to phone Sutton Bonnington and a man would come and inject the cow. If another cow was in season, he would see to that one at the same time. We had to pay for the service of course but it was cheaper than having to keep a bull and safer and less work as well.

There was a move in the 1950s to eradicate T.B. (tuberculosis). The government had said that they would pay an extra fourpence a gallon for milk from tuberculin tested cows. My father arranged for our herd to be tested straight away. The vet injected the cows in the neck, two injections about three inches apart. He returned three days later and repeated the exercise. If there was not the right reaction, we had to get rid of that cow straight away. There was no compensation. From then on, the herd was tested every year. We had to be strict with them, not allowing them to stray or mix with untested stock. It wasn't long before most of the other farmers had their herds T.B. tested. The public demanded it. Now all cows are T.B. tested. Tuberculosis is almost eradicated.

We had an Alfa Laval milking machine since 1943. Mr. Gemmell came round to see to it in his Hillman car. He arrived one day when the dairy maid was getting married. Her sweetheart was in the army and had two day's leave. Mr. Gemmell emptied everything out of his car and drove her down to the Church.

• • • • • •

My father is a farmer and we have a herd of 60 cows. They're all milked by machine. They're milked twice a day and when they come into the shed, they go to their own stall. We wash down their udders and attach the milking machine to their four teats. These pull and suck. The milk goes along a pipe to a glass tank. There is a computer on the machine that measures the amount of milk each cow has given and then releases the exact amount of high protein food for that animal. The milk lorry comes round each day and collects the milk. All

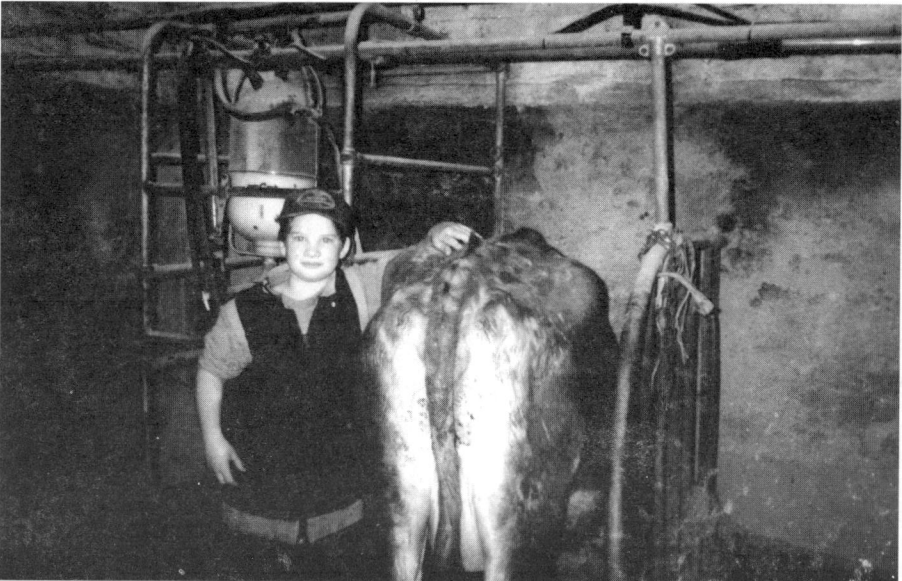

milk is pasteurized, i.e. brought up to a certain temperature to kill bacteria. We are paid sixteen and a halfpence a litre for milk. Two years ago we received 25p a litre. A good milking cow gives 6,000 litres per annum so this reduction in payment has meant a big loss to dairy farmers.

I now leave the calves with the cows and rear them for beef. I sell them at 18 months. I use the continental bulls. They produce leaner meat and that's what the public demands.

B.S.E. was a tragedy. Although there is no proof, it is a possibility that humans can get B.S.E. from eating 'contaminated' beef. I think we over-reacted in Britain. All countries have this problem but it hasn't had the publicity that we had here. We had to have perfectly healthy animals destroyed. If they are older than 30 months they have to be destroyed; they cannot go into the human food chain. It nearly broke my heart. The public seems to think farmers don't care about their animals but they couldn't be more wrong. Ours are all part of the family. They all have names and we know their characters. The bottom has fallen out of the market when we were just picking up from the B.S.E. scare. I got 90p a kilo for mine at market last week. Last month it was 75p a kilo. The price is going down again. The problem is that we're bringing too much beef in from abroad. There's too much Irish beef coming in. They don't have to meet all the stringent conditions that we do.

I'm 10 and I'm going to be a farmer when I grow up. My Dad says I should look for another career because there's not enough money in farming now. I'm going to keep cattle. I bought my first calf at Newark Market last week, a Belgian Blue heifer. I'd saved up for it. The man wanted £15.00 for it. I know you don't give people what they ask, so I said I'd give him £12.00 and he said, "No way," so I walked away. He called after me and said I could have it for £14.00 and he would give me £1.00 for luck. So I got it for £13.00. I am going to save for another. I'm going to have my own herd and I'll probably keep some cows to milk.

• • • • • •

My Grandfather grew hops but gave up in 1914. He grew teazles for the Lancashire mills at the turn of the century. That's a crop you never hear of today

but you often find teazles and hops growing wild along the hedgerows as a reminder of the crops that used to be grown.

We would rotate the crops to keep the soil in good order, wheat, roots, oats, clover in that order. We grew mustard (a green crop) which we ploughed in to enrich the soil. We used the manure from the crew yards to spread on the land to add nutrition to the soil. I can remember old Ernie Robinson towing the muck spreader down the road when something went wrong with it and it sprayed all the cars coming up behind with manure. Regulations are coming in where we can only use treated waste on the soil. Untreated waste carries pathogens which can be put into the soil. We use fertilisers instead.

Mr. Stephenson had the farm where the gravel pits are now. It was good sandy soil, just right for vegetables. He had a contract with the canning factory. He grew mainly carrots, beetroot, onions and French beans for them. They couldn't be just any kind of vegetable, they had to be just right for the canning factory. They wanted baby carrots although they would sometimes want bigger ones that could be sliced and canned.

I worked at Coningsby Airfield and we moved into Kirkby in 1950. I would often come home from work, have my tea and go straight out to work on the land. Mr. Stephenson could generally find a job that needed doing. One day he asked me to single beet. There was a young airman who had come to help as well and he did not know what he was doing. He hadn't singled beet before. I was at the end of my row before he had put one foot in front of the other. He tried to keep up with me and he got into a right mess. All his rows had to be done again.

Then Mr. Poucher from Woodhall way asked me to chop out and single some sugar beet for him. He had side hoes on his tractor and went down the rows first. I was paid piecework, £12.00 an acre and I did four acres for him. That was good money when you think that the average working wage was three pounds a week.

We don't keep any stock now except for some farmyard hens. We grow crops, mainly wheat, oil seed rape and linseed. I took over from my father twelve years ago. He never grew any oilseed crops. He grew kale for the cattle, potatoes and some wheat and barley.

These are Britain's main crops.

Wheat	41%
Barley	27%
Oilseed rape	9%
Peas and beans	4%
Sugar beet	4%
Fruit and veg	4%
Potatoes	3%
Other	8%

There is so much more scientific knowledge and practice in farming than there was forty years ago. The farmer has to keep in touch with all these advances if he is to stay in business.

Food plants are being genetically engineered. Plant breeding has always existed i.e. one plant has been crossed with another to produce better plants. Corn used to grow to a metre and a half. Now that we use less straw, we have wheat plants with shorter stalks. The plant breeders have crossed different wheat plants to produce this. Genetically engineered plants are where genetic engineering is used to take out genes and segments of DNA from one species e.g. fish and put them into another species e.g. tomato.

A good example of this has been in China where the main (and often the only) diet is rice. This has lead to premature blindness because of the lack of vitamin A in the diet. Daffodils are strong in this vitamin so the gene from daffodils has been combined with the rice and the dietary problem has virtually disappeared.

We have our soil anaylsed. That is an added cost. We add fertilisers to the soil, either in autumn or spring. Where the land is heavy, we use triple super phosphate. On lighter land, like sandy soil, we use potash. We try to correct the deficiencies that show up in the soil tests.

Growing crops take the nutrients from the soil and these have to be replaced. There is an index that measures the nutrients. 4-5 means that the soil is rich in nutrients and nothing needs to be added. 2-3 means that fertilisers have to be added to balance the nutrients.

In 1995, we were told that we were producing too much wheat and we are paid not to produce crops on some of our land. This is known as set aside. We call that lazy farming.

Drainage is another aspect of good soil management. The roots of a wheat plant will go six feet (1.8 metres) into the ground. If the plant becomes waterlogged it dies. We always kept the ditches in good order but part of our land still got waterlogged so we got a grant and had drainage pipes laid in 1950. The drainage pipes are situated just above the water table and they are covered with porous soil. The pipes are laid with a gap every two chains and they take the surplus water away. It was worth it. Our yield per acre increased. The subsidies for drainage were withdrawn in 1986.

•••••••

Ploughing, drilling and harvesting has always been our year. We used three horses to pull the single furrow plough but in the south fields, where the soil is lighter, we only had to use two. Down by the river where it's blow away sandy soil, they could get away with one. It took a day to plough an acre. It took me the whole week to plough our five acre field. I liked working with the horses. They were such gentle giants. I was fourteen when I started work. I used to go down to the stable at half past four in the morning to fetch the horses ready for their day's work. I couldn't reach their heads and

I had to stand on the manger to get their head collars on.

The advantage of a cart horse was that it understood what you said. It would stop when you told it. They were living things. Tractors aren't the same. They all had their own characters those old cart horses. Well we had this horse and it would stand up on its hind legs and that was a frightening sight when you were underneath it. Well I didn't know my wife that well. She was my girlfriend then. We were out one day, me managing the plough and she was leading the horse when something startled him because up on to his hind legs he went. He was ready to make a bolt for it. I shouted to her to hold the horse and she was hanging on to it for dear life. She said afterwards that I was more concerned about the horse than her but she still agreed to be Mrs. Spikins when I got round to asking her.

We had a horse, Dolly we called her and she was a real steady animal except when she took it in her head to go her own way and there was no stopping her. I finished up with her half way through our neighbour's back door one day, loaded cart and all when she decided to turn right through his hedge rather than turn into the gateway.

My brother in law worked on a farm with a horse that the farmer had hired. It was a big black horse. When my brother in law sat down by the hedge to eat his lunch, the old horse goes and sits down beside him, sat right up on his bottom, just like an old man. From then on he used to sit beside my brother in law every lunchtime until he had to go back to the stables.

It was usually a two man job ploughing a field, one to lead the horse and one to manage the plough, but if you had a good ploughman, he would do the job single-handed. There was a seat on which you sat on the plough but when you got to the end of the furrow and had to turn round, you'd be leaning out to one side so that you were almost touching the ground to pull it round.

It was hard to stop a cart horse when it bolted. The only way was to pull hard on one side of its reins.

The man from Ebbington Bridge used to bring the shire stallion round to seed the mares. He was only a little fellow with bandy legs and it was a hard job steadying the stallion especially when he got the smell of the mares but he managed it alright. I loved working with the horses. You were working with something alive. They were like part of the family.

The tractors weren't the same. They didn't have a soul. I wasn't the only one who shed a tear when they took the horses away to be shot. The tractors had taken their place, hadn't they? I can remember buying our first tractor. I saw them at the first Royal Agricultural Show after the war. It was at Lincoln in 1948. Harry Ferguson had a stand there with his tractors with the new hydraulic system. They developed that from the wartime aeroplanes. They were small lightweight tractors with self starters. Until then tractors had to be started with a starting handle and they took a lot of strength. There were many people who injured their wrists when the handle kicked back when they were starting a tractor. Harry Ferguson's tractors had the same engine as the Standard Vanguard car and there were all the implements to go with them. I didn't buy one then but I thought about it. Henry Gill was a farmer by way of being a hobby, (he was a jeweller in Horncastle by trade), but he had this land in Kirkby and he bought one of those tractors at the show. I bought mine the year after. Well it changed my life straight away. There was no early morning rising to prepare the horses. A turn of the key and the tractor was ready. There was one man to take the plough now instead of two and it could plough two or three times what a horse and single furrow plough could do. It was the same with everything.

They didn't have any use for the heavy horses any more and they were expensive to keep. Then one November, the master told us to pull the carts and drays out of the shed and put them on the bonfire. That was the end of farming for me. I didn't have my heart in it. I gave up working on the land and took a job driving.

My father was killed three months before I was born. That was in the First World War. My mother married again some time after and we moved to Yorkshire but I never settled there so I came down to Lincolnshire and got a job on a smallholding. I was lucky to get it. Times were hard in the 1930s. There wasn't much work to be had but it had been much worse in Yorkshire. After a while I got a job with Mr. H.B. Hundleby from Orby Bank driving the old iron horses, the traction engines. They were wonderful machines. I loved working on them.

We would take the traction engines for ploughing, two engines in the field with a rope stretched out between us pulling the plough. We would be away a week or more at a time and we lived in a caravan which we pulled behind the engine. It wasn't a caravan like they have today, it looked more like a railway carriage but it was comfortable enough. We had a stove in it to cook a meal but I preferred to get home when I could.

I did threshing mostly and it was dirty, dusty work especially in the spring when the corn had been lying in the stacks for months. Before the war, farmers generally built their stacks in crew yards but during the war, they were advised to spread the stacks to stop them firing.

Traction engines travelled at 4 m.p.h. – 6 if they were on springs. They often broke down but we knew how to repair them, We would take them to the farm and set them up on the night before we started threshing then I would cycle home for the night. I often cycled twenty miles out to a farm and twenty miles back at night and we worked seven days a week for £2.00, threshing during the week and washing out the machine and cleaning it on the Sunday. We were threshing down at Kirkby. We'd done two stacks and I hadn't seen a rat run out of them so I told the farmer I wouldn't put the engine alongside the stack the night before, I'd wait until the morning. When I did the rats poured out. I'd never seen rats like it. The farm was over run with rats.

• • • • • •

I was cutting the grass in front of the cottage when Mr. Brock stopped and asked me if I could give him a hand with the threshing. Mr. Brock was in his seventies then, a tall man who wore knee breeches and gaiters. Most of the farmers dressed like that. If you didn't wear them, you made sure you tied the bottoms of your trousers with string to stop the rats running up them when you were out threshing. Harold Thompson had a rat run up his trouser leg when he wasn't expecting it and you've never seen such a dance in your life. There was only one old man at the other end of the village that still wore a smock and it was always white so I don't expect he did much work. No, I don't know what they wore under their smocks. I never asked them. The same as the Scots wear under their kilts I suppose. Mr. Brock was so bow-legged, a pig could have run between his legs and he wouldn't have noticed it. There were ten men on a threshing gang and we would clear a stack in a day if we could but it was hot dusty work. There were two men on the stack, pulling the sheaves from the stack and throwing them across to the elevator. This would bring them up to where I was standing on the threshing machine. Sometimes we wouldn't use the elevator. The men on the stack would throw the sheaves across to the thresher. My job was catching the sheaves, cutting the rope off them and feeding them in to the drum. You had to be careful. It you slipped, your leg could go through the slats to where the knives were. They were razor sharp. There were many farm cats that met their end that way, chasing mice and getting caught up in the blades. Andrew Siddons was on the stack and he started sending up the sheaths faster than I could catch them. He was in a hurry to get home but I couldn't feed them into the drum any faster or I would have jammed up the cutters. I shouted to him to slow down but they seemed to come faster than ever. He was breaking the rhythm. 'What shall I do with him?' Mr. Brock asked. 'Sack him' I said, 'or swap him for his father.' So he was sent to clean the chaff and we got on with the job at a decent speed.

Clarence Siddons asked if he could take a couple of hours off on the Saturday. He had to go to his sister in law's wedding. We didn't expect to see him back but they must have given him plenty to drink because a couple of hours later, we could hear him singing as he came along the path. Mr. Brock told him he'd better go home for a while and sleep it off but he didn't seem to hear and the next thing was that he was climbing up the side of the threshing machine trying to reach me. He reckoned he could do my job for me and we had the devil of a job keeping him away. We didn't dare let him up alongside me because he could have slipped his legs through those slats as easy as kiss your father. We had to push him off in the end and he fell quite heavily but it didn't seem to bother him. He took to singing again and staggered back towards the village. Clearing the chaff was the worst job of all. The corn came down through a riddle and the chaff came out of the side and it had to be kept clear. You could hardly breathe for the dust. The corn was left on the elevator and went up through a chopper and into the bags. There were five sacks. The good corn went into the first two sacks. Chicken feed went into the next two and the last sack was mainly weeds and waste. Two men would clear and stack the straw and two would see to the sacks, taking them to store in the barn. They were heavy when they were full. 18 stone of wheat, 16 stone of barley or 12 stone of oats. We used a hicking barrow to lift the sacks on to our shoulders. These were barrows that stood up straight with two handles. There was a small platform on which you placed the sack and by turning a handle, a chain would lift the platform to a height where we could manage to get it on to our shoulders more easily. Grinto, the German POW who worked down at Spikins farm was only a little fellow but he was muscular and he could lift the sack right up from the ground without any trouble and carry it up the steps to the store. There was a little chap up at Mr. Brock's no taller than three pea pots and he could carry a sack of corn up the steps faster than any of the other men. He was so small it looked like the sack had grown a couple of feet and was running up the steps on its own. Farms have forklift trucks now. Men don't have to carry the weights they used to. There's only one man needed to drive a combine harvester and that does it all, the reaping and the threshing. It was very different when I started farming.

I always took my holidays at harvest time. Everyone I knew did. Everyone who could help came including the children. The farmers prayed for good weather as the corn ripened. If it was left standing in the field too long it would become overripe or if there was too much rain, it would go mouldy. They didn't have the dryers that they have today.

The farmer tested the corn to see if it was ready by rubbing two or three ears in the palms of his hands. If the husks rubbed off easily, he knew it was ready to cut. We cut the first width round the field with scythes. It took a bit of mastering, swinging a scythe. You had to get them balanced right. Once that was done, we brought in the reapers. They were horse drawn cutters. We followed behind, gathering the corn and tying it in sheaves. Others following behind us picked up the sheaves and put them in stooks, six or eight sheaves to a stook. These were stood ears up and the stalks spread out so that they would dry better.

Then they brought in sail reapers. They were the same as the old reapers except that they had four large caravan sails that went round like windmill sails collecting the corn in to sheaf sized bundles. That saved a lot of work and it saved a lot more when the binders came in. These were reapers that tied the sheaves before they pushed them out so all we had to do was pick them up and put them in stooks. That was the idea but the binders were always breaking down and there were many times we had to gather the corn in as if it were a hay crop. Farmers weren't experienced with machinery. They would leave the binder out in the field for best part of the year and then expect it to work straight away. They seldom thought about cleaning or oiling them.

The sheaves were heavy but they became lighter as they dried out. It was hot, thirsty work but it was the same for everyone. They were happy days, happy that the harvest was being gathered in because that was the most important time of the year for the farmers and happy to be working with friends and neighbours. We used to leave bottles of cold tea in the corners of the fields and stop to have a drink as we went round. There's nothing like cold tea for slaking one's thirst. Bert reckoned cider was better and he kept a few bottles for the harvest and real strong stuff it was. It may have quenched his thirst but it didn't do much for his brain and he was as likely to stand the sheaves the wrong way up by the end on the day and we had to get a child to follow him round to keep him on the right path.

We used to have time off from school for the harvest. We used to help carry the sheaves or fetch and carry for the men. I always liked it when we stopped for lunch. Men took their own, generally wrapped in a cloth. It was always the same, a hunk of bread, a piece of cheese and an onion. Out would come the knives, the same knives that they used for cutting the string or repairing the binder and they would cut into the food. They never thought about washing the knives although they sometimes wiped them on their trousers. During the war, the farmers had extra rations during harvest. They had to make sure the workers in the field were fed.

We children had to take the rabbits back to the cottages for the women to skin. All the time that the corn was being cut, rabbits would be running out of the standing corn to the hedges for cover and everyone seemed to be trying to kill them. I like rabbits. I didn't like touching dead rabbits. Tom cut a stick out of the hedges, fastened six rabbits on that so I could go home with the stick over my shoulder. I didn't have to touch them. Rabbits had a value. We sold the skins and ate the meat. During the war, when meat was strictly rationed, we could make a bit of money from rabbits.

As the reaper got to the last of the standing corn, everyone would stop for a few minutes. Then we were spread round this final square and the men and boys armed themselves with sticks mainly although some had guns. The dogs were brought up. Then the reaper started up again and all hell was let loose. The rabbits ran. There were hundreds and hundreds of them. They had all been retreating to the 'safety' of the centre of the field. We had been waiting in silence, then, as the first rabbits ran, we started shouting and banging tin lids. The dogs were running and jumping and killing rabbits and so were the men and the boys. It was awful yet it was exciting and it was a way of life. At least the rabbits were killed without suffering.

Rabbits were a problem. There were thousands and thousands of rabbits and they ate the growing crops. You couldn't go anywhere in the countryside without seeing rabbits in the fields. Down at Jericho Farm, there were great bare patches where the crops were eaten down to the ground. He had acres on which he couldn't grow crops because the rabbits were clearing them as fast as he planted them. Then in 1953, myxamatosis was introduced. This was an infection spread by rabbit fleas. It was dreadful. It seemed that overnight the rabbits that dotted the fields were dead and dying. They didn't have the strength to move but sat there with swollen heads and unseeing eyes. There were thousands of them. In some fields there were so many that it was difficult to walk between them. The loss of the rabbits helped farmers to produce more food but it had a bad effect on country living. There were no rabbit's skins to sell, no rabbits to eat. Animals that had survived mainly on rabbits, like buzzards and badgers also began to suffer, the countryside became empty almost overnight.

The sheaves stood out in the fields until they were dry enough to stack. If the weather was damp, they could be left out for weeks before they were gathered in. One year there was snow on the ground before we brought the last of the corn in. They were loaded on to the farm carts and taken back to the farm yard. There was quite an art in loading them. You had to put them on the cart ears innermost and you would need a man on top to tread them down and make sure that they were knitted in, one sheath with the next. It was hard work lifting the sheaves on to the cart. It was a good pitchfork length and your arms would ache from lifting them. If you didn't get the load balanced, you were likely to lose it on the way back to the farm. That happened with the first load I ever helped load. There was nothing for it. We had to take the whole lot off and start again. There was another day we lost the load but that was different. The horse bolted with an almost full load. She was standing there as quiet as ever while we loaded and suddenly, she was off. Right through the hedge she went, cart and all, scattering sheaves as she went and through the next one and all. She would have finished up in the river if the cart hadn't caught in the hedge. We guessed she'd been bitten by a horse fly to make her go off like that.

We children often sat on top of the load and travelled back to the farm but I never felt safe there. The corn could be slippery and there was nothing to hold on to but we always went back that way when the last load went back. They decorated the horses' headbands with twigs of oak then. It was a custom that went out when we started using tractors.

You had to know what you were doing when you built a stack. The heads always pointed into the centre and the sheaves always had to fit in with the next one. A well built stack was solid. You had to make sure the stack was dry. If any of the sheaves were wet, you threw them out. The top of the stack was thatched to stop the rain penetrating. Ropes were stretched across this thatch to hold it and pegged down with willow pegs. Damp could turn into fire damp and the whole stack would burst into flames without any warning. We used to test the temperature of the stacks regularly by pushing a long metal pole into the centre of the stack. If it was hot when it came out, then we dismantled the whole stack straight away. You couldn't risk fire in the farmyard. When we finished the stack, we would put wire mesh round the base to keep the rats out.

After the corn had been cut, the gleaners came in with their buckets and bags to gather any corn that had fallen on to the ground. The widows and the needy went in first, then anyone from the village could go. Mother had a sackcloth apron which she filled with corn and when it was full, she tipped the contents into a sack. She'd collect enough corn to feed our hens through to the next harvest.

The gleaners came into our fields when we had harvested the peas. 19 stone of peas to a sack. That took some lifting. We used to send our peas to Theodore's, the pea merchants in Louth. My sister in law worked there before she married. You should have seen the pea rooms with all the girls in their white aprons sorting the peas. They all had to be sorted by hand.

Yes my mother went gleaning peas. We were fair drowned in peas. She used to spread them out and dry them in the sun. She kept some to feed us in the winter, the rest went to feed the hens and the pig.

The birds helped with the gleaning. There were flocks of birds that descended on to the fields. Sparrows seemed to fly in miniature clouds but it's the linnets I miss most. You would always see them round the haystacks. They're such dainty little birds and I miss the call of the lapwing. Theirs was the call of the spring for me. We used to collect lapwing eggs to eat but we never touched them after April 14th. After that, their eggs were for them to breed. The sound of the skylark is another summer sound I miss but there were more grass fields when I was a child, better conditions for the birds and more food for them to find. There isn't much waste with modern farming.

There's not much waste when I cut the corn. There is a computer in my combine harvester that keeps me informed on the yield, the moisture content, anything I want to know. If there is a fault on the machine, then a loud buzz will tell me and the part that needs attention will show up on the screen. They're wonder machines compared with the old reapers my father used to use. But we have to pay for these wonder machines. A combine harvester costs up to £250,000. There's no way the average farmer can afford that kind of money so I'm like the others. I either borrow from the bank or I lease my machinery. Self-propelled sugar beet harvesters are in the same sort of cost bracket, and potato harvesters are £100,000. We may save money because we don't have to pay the wages and, of course the machines are more efficient, but the banks are greedier. I always used to grow potatoes, I had a contract with the crisp factory but they let me down a couple of times, didn't want the potatoes when I'd grown them. They paid what they had agreed but I lost the profit I'd expected. Now I grow mainly corn and oilseed crops. I occasionally keep some corn back for seed but

Modern farm machinery and buildings

Modern farm machinery

Modern farm machinery and buildings

it isn't the same quality of that that I buy in. Bought seed has been treated against disease. I sow 12 stone to an acre of wheat and the seed is expensive. I had to pay £400 a ton for spring wheat two years ago but it's generally less that that. When I harvest the wheat, I get about three and a half tons to an acre according to the quality of the land. When we first went into the common market in 1982, I was harvesting one and three quarter ton to the acre. I get £68.00 a ton for basic wheat. That's not the quality wheat. You grow different kinds of wheat, seed wheat for milling wheat, that's the best quality and used for bread. Then there's biscuit wheat and feed wheat and Durham wheat. That's used for pastas.

Modern farm machinery is very sophisticated.

If something is wrong with the modern tractor it will flash on the dashboard, and the engine may cut. The farmer cannot fix this so he has to call the mechanic and he will come out and plug his lap-top in and it will tell him what is wrong with the tractor and then the mechanic will fix it.

A carrot lifter has two cameras in the machine connected to screens in the tractors so the driver can see what's going on in the lifter.

A combine can have a cutter bar 30ft wide (9.15m) and a grain tank capacity of 9,500 litres.

Some combines have a printer fitted which prints out the yield over the different areas of the field. This information is fed into the office computer which then produces a field map in grids showing where the yields vary. The farmer can then have the relevant areas of the field soil tested to show which nutrients are lacking in the soil. When the soil test results are produced they are put on a smart card. The smart card is then put into the tractor which is fitted with a fertiliser spreader. The computer in the tractor then regulates how much fertiliser is spread. If one area is lacking in certain nutrients, it will put more fertiliser on this area and reduce the rate where a smaller amount is needed. This is a very accurate way of farming as individual areas of the field are treated as needed. However it is extremely expensive and although most farmers would like to use this system, farm incomes are low at the moment and the cost is high.

• • • • • •

We always had poultry on the farm, for our own needs. There were always hens scratching in the yard and geese round the pond. We had ducks for a while but they were always finding their way to the river and we were having to go and collect them from two or three miles downstream. We'd never heard of battery cages. Our hens were free to roam and there weren't any additives in the eggs we ate.

We moved into Kirkby on Bain in 1950. We bought a smallholding from Bob Croft. We bought 200 day old Rhode Island chicks from Sterlings at Woodhall Spa. We reared them in incubators until they began to feather up. Then we put them in deep litter houses. They started to lay at twenty weeks. We had them outside then, in pens and they pecked the nutrients from the ground as well as eating the corn and household scraps I fed them. I boiled up the potato peel and gave them that. We didn't waste anything. We gave them grit as well otherwise they would have laid soft shelled eggs. We had 300 hens altogether and they would each lay 5 or 6 eggs a week except when they were moulting.

Mike asked me to collect the eggs when he went off to work. He'd been brought up on a farm so he was used to animals. I wasn't sure of the hens. They pecked and their beaks were sharp. When Mike came home from work there were only two eggs in the bucket and I'd taken an age getting them. He was not pleased. He said that if we didn't collect the eggs, the hens would start eating them. I worked out a plan. I found a stick with a Y shaped end and I held their necks firm while I fetched out the eggs they were sitting on. They were a bit disturbed when they saw the stick but they soon settled down. We washed the eggs and packed them in boxes that held 30 dozen and the egg marketing lorry collected them every Monday morning.

We only ever had chicken as a treat when I was a child and a goose for Christmas. We kept hens for the eggs. Now we often have chicken but they don't have as much taste as the ones we had when we were children but then they're reared differently.

My Dad has a chicken farm. We have two sheds, one of which has 2 sides, 4,000 chickens on each side. They are Loman Browns on one side and Hisex on the other. We have 1,850 chickens in the other shed and they are all Loman Brown. The hens are kept in battery cages and we collect 6,000 eggs a day from the first shed and 1,660 from the second. A lorry collects the eggs but we let Lodge Farm have some and they sell them for us. The hens are contented. The eggs roll down to a shelf when they lay them so they are clean.

Regulations are coming in to ensure that hens can perch. This means they will need more room and so eggs will be more expensive and farmers will not be able to compete with imported eggs. Eggs are imported from Asia and South America where they do not have the restrictions that we have in England.

My Dad works with chickens. They produce chicken for meat and they are kept on deep litter. My father has to wear a mask when he goes in the shed because it is dusty. The chicks come in as day olds and are ready for the table at 35-49 days when they are about 2 kilograms in weight – the EEC have recommended the maximum stocking ratio and they follow those rules. They also give the recommended feed – they are very strict about the conditions in which they keep the birds but they have to compete with foreign imports. 40% of frozen chickens sold in this country comes from countries like Brazil and Thailand where they do not have such strict regulations and do not pay their labour so much. All the British meat products are regularly tested and are of good quality.

● ● ● ● ● ●

I worked with trees all my life. You have to know what you're doing when you fell a tree or even a heavy branch. They can fall the wrong way if you don't. We used a two-man saw, seven foot long with a handhold at each end. We'd start on a tree at eight o'clock of a morning and we'd still be working on it at five o'clock at night. When we had a good tree that was wanted for furniture like a walnut, we didn't cut that down. We dug it out. The best wood is often the base of a trunk and that can go down four or five feet into the ground. There's no tap root to a walnut. It has four or five main roots that hold it in place. We'd find these roots some way out from the tree and we'd go at them with an axe, getting nearer the trunk all the time. Sometimes these roots would be as thick as a tree trunk. Once we'd found and cut through these main roots, then we'd start on the small roots that were holding the tree firm. Sometimes, a root, no bigger that a straw would be holding it firm.

Fred Bailey is a champion plasher. Plashing is an art as well as a craft and, in modern times, it is a dying art. A good thorn hedge is still not only a pleasure to look at, but also the most practical "fence" for keeping animals where you want them!

At the age of 74 Fred plashed a 120 yard thorn hedge at 'Cortlands'. It had been allowed to grow unchecked for 10 years and had reached a height of some 25ft. It needed expert attention to save it since it had become overgrown with elder, brambles, nettles etc; was undermined by rabbits and moles, and had joined forces with another parallel hedge growing 10ft away over its full length.

I reckoned that clearing the undergrowth alone was a six month job. Fred did it in 2 days!

We were paid piecework, twopence halfpenny a cubic foot for hardwood, a penny halfpenny for soft. I had my first chainsaw in 1943. I soon put that on one side and went back to the old handsaw. Well we'd spend the best part of the day keeping the thing running. When the chainsaws came in, they wanted to reduce payment, twopence a cubic foot for hardwood and less than a penny for soft.

We were felling a walnut across at the rectory and just as I swung my axe, I saw something glinting in the sunlight and I caught it with the blade. I scrabbled through the debris till I found this thing and there it is – a King George the First coin and there's the cut my axe made. That will tell you the age of the tree. They used to put a coin under a tree when they planted it. I don't think they bother with that sort of thing nowadays. I've got a whole bagful of these coins I picked up when we felled a tree.

On the reserve

My Dad helps Terry on Kirby Moor. Terry cuts down the trees with a chainsaw. My sister Abby and I saw off the branches and burn them. Then my Dad cuts the rest up for logs. We take the logs we want, then Terry sells the rest for firewood. Terry clears an acre in the day. He only cuts down the self seeded birch. He doesn't touch the oak trees because there aren't as many oaks as birch trees and the oaks are much older. Terry wants to encourage the heather to grow and doesn't want to get crowded out with birch. The reserve at Kirkby Moor is the largest remnant of the once extensive heathlands of the Woodhall district.

I like going through the plantation because it is exciting. In the war, the copse was at the end of the runway for Woodhall Airfield and you can still find signs of the war amongst the trees. There are old wartime buildings and concrete aprons where the aeroplanes were hidden beneath the trees and other places that were bomb dumps. You can see and hear aircraft flying out of Coningsby and I often look at them and wonder what it must have been like in the wartime when they flew overhead.

Trees are harvested like any other crop. Trees are grown for a special purpose. Most of the wood used for furniture and household goods is imported. It's mainly conifers that are grown in the plantation today. They are cut down and cut to length and left in piles waiting to be picked up. They mostly go to pulp mills to be made into paper or they may go to commercial timber firms.

Do you remember the willow plantation? The owner grew them mainly for osiers but he had some cricket bat willows as well. They used to make their own baskets and things from the willow. I've still got an old eel trap he made down in the shed. There were plenty of eels in the river and they made good eating.

We are planting trees on our nature reserve which is at the far end of our playing field.

We made it because nature, environment and birds are things Mr Douglas (the Headteacher) wants to look after, I think it was a good idea.

• • • • • •

When you come to Kirkby on Bain from Coningsby, you pass some lakes where all kinds of birds can be seen. These are the old gravel pits.

The gravel pits opened in 1950. Further land has been bought and continuous production has been maintained for 50 years. The current Chairman is Mr David Jones, son of the founder of the company which started in 1934 to supply aggregates for the extension of Boston docks. Demand increased during the war years for building Coningsby and other Lincolnshire Airfields.

You can find fossils and stones in the gravel pits. Before the gravel pits were there it was farmland. My great grandad, Mr Stephenson was the manager of the farm and my dad was born there.

The farm was called Castle View Farm because you could see Tattershall Castle. There were many types of trees e.g. Willows, Silver Birch, Fir.

Sand and gravel are used for building. It is excavated, extracted, washed and screened. Then it is graded, processed and stockpiled until it is collected by tipper lorries for delivery to construction sites and ready mix concrete plants. The company has a bagging plant which bags sand and gravel into 50kg and 1,000kg bags.

The three washing screening plants are loaded with as dug material (ballast) which is washed. Silt is extracted and deposited in lagoons. The clean sand is separated into soft sand (for mortar in bricklaying) and grit sand (used in concrete).

1954, Ron Dixon waiting for a load of sand or gravel to deliver to customers in the area including the local aerodromes

Digging out sand and ballast. The top soil and blue clay has been removed and is stored and replaced when mining has ceased

Part of the cost of extracting gravel has to reflect the high cost of reinstatement of the land, here we see some of the plant required in that process

Reclaimed pits - infill site made into a nature reserve. Ornithologists come from all over the country to the lakes to view migrating wildfowl that use the lakes as a stopping off point

Worked out gravel pit before the present owners took over

The same gravel pit showing present reclamation scheme. Eventually this will be green meadow for sheep to graze - note the lighter blue clay and the darker top soil onto which grass will be sown

A newly created lake

The topsoil is generally 500mm thick and the seams of sand and gravel vary in depth and beneath this is a heavy layer of stiff blue clay which holds the water. The water table varies but it generally needs pumping before the lower levels can be excavated. The seams are generally sandier to the west. The excavated soil is approximately

Silt	3%
Fine	57-72%
Coarse	25-40%
Oversize	5%

Land is being quarried south of Kirkby village formally farmed by Mr John Leggate, on land north of Tattershall Thorpe Village formerly farmed by Mr Norman Leggate and on land to the east of Kirkby formerly owned by Mr Tom Scholey of Tumby.

The firm offered employment to the local people. In 1994, when it celebrated its Golden Jubilee, David Jones paid tribute to the manager, Keith Robinson who had worked for them for 41 years as well as Ruby Hempshall, Les Wilkinson, Roy and Fred Hempshall and Ron Dixon who had clocked up 225 years service between them.

The Company is applying for permission to excavate sand and gravel from land to the south of the village and from land between the River Bain and Horncastle Canal. There are many requirements that they have to fulfil today to make sure that the environment is not affected adversely. They have to consult with Parish, District and County Councils, Environment Agencies, Archeological and Museum Authorities, wildlife Agencies and the Ministry of Defence because of Coningsby airfield birdstrike safe guarding issues.

There has been an increased interest in the archeological information from our area and evidence of Neolithic and Saxon inhabitants living near Kirkby on Bain have been deposited in the County's Museum in Lincoln. Evidence of dinosaurs roaming the area have also been found and the excavators have often dug up bones from that area.

The worked out areas are reused. Some is restored to agricultural land by infilling with quarry waste, drained and topsoiled. The County Council uses some of the pits for landfill, dumping local household refuse. Originally this was to be filled in to the original field level but now it is built up into a dome to allow rainwater to run off and not enter the stored waste.

Part of the land was sold to the Lincolnshire Trust for Wildlife who have established a Reserve there with bird watching facilities. Lakes have been established in worked out pits which large numbers of geese, duck and wildfowl visit. BUT quarries are dangerous places and must only be entered when accompanied by a member of the quarry staff. The sides of the lakes are steep – please keep away.

THE FUTURE

In the next century, I think all the farmers will have computers and everything will be done by machines. The fields will be marked ABCDE and the farmers will press a button and a machine will come out and go to that field. They won't need drivers. There won't be animals in the fields. They will be kept indoors. All the fields will be used for crops. Anything that takes nutrition from the soil, like hedges will have disappeared. Trees will be grown like a field of wheat because they will be needed for fuel. We will need more houses and bigger ones. Kirkby will be as big as Boston.

Farmers will be the most important people in the world because there will be lots more people on the earth but there won't be any more land. The animals will all be cloned too. Perhaps people will be cloned too. All the ladies will look like the Queen and the men will look like Mr Douglas.

Pupils of Kirkby on Bain School taken outside St Mary's Church, Kirkby on Bain: 1956 or 1957.
Most of the children lived in the village. Today only 17 of the 86 children on roll live in the village.
Back row left to right: Queena Smith, Dorothy Wright, Joan Roberts, Hannah Smith, Pearl Ingham Jean Adams, Bryan Roberts, Jean Dixon, Jean Ingham.
Middle row l to r: Griffin ?, Jim Wright, Mick Prime, Barbara Bennett, Josie Rainforth, Jim Cutting, Roy Atkin, Greta Maddy.
Front Row l to r: Shirley Adams, Elizabeth Skelton, Derek Allen, Loll Bennett, Dick Rainforth, Harold Maddy